Vintage

Vintage

A Play in Two Acts

By

Rik Lonsdale and John Nash

Copyright © 2024 by Rik Lonsdale and John Nash

www.riklonsdale.com
All Rights Reserved.

No part of this work may be used or reproduced by any means, graphic, electronic, or mechanical, including photocopying, recording, taping, or by any information storage retrieval system, or by any Artificial Intelligence scanning, scraping, or learning, without the written permission of the publisher except in the case of brief quotations embodied in critical articles and reviews.

All rights in this play are reserved. Applications to perform must be made, before any rehearsals begin to, the authors at rik.lonsdale@outlook.com

This is a work of fiction. All names, characters, places, and incidents are the product of the authors' imaginations and any resemblance to actual persons, living or dead, events, or locales is entirely coincidental.

ISBN 978-1-7392823-6-3

Cover artwork by Rob Adams robadams@treeshark.com

Dedicated to:
All the members of COMPACT who first
brought "Vintage" to life on 18th October 2024

Setting

The setting is a charity shop in a run-down small town.

The stage is divided into two. Stage R is the main 'shop', stage L is the 'Storeroom' Each can be lit separately. The shop half is larger than the storeroom half.

In the shop down SR is a translucent door, the main entry to the shop, mid SR is a small counter with till. Centre up stage is a small desk and chair. Down SL is the coveted 'vintage' rail. Up SL is a blank door into:

The storeroom. SL in the storeroom is a sink and kettle with tea things. Elsewhere is a mish-mash of donations and general clutter hiding a work table SR. There may be a couple of stools. There are never more than two characters in the storeroom.

Cast of Characters

Grace   Woman in her later years

Clarissa   Woman in her later years

Ruth   Woman in her later years

Stephanie   Woman aged 19

Betty   Customer 1 a woman in her later years

Pearl   Customer 2 a woman in her later years

Meg   Customer 3 a woman in her later years

Surveyor   Age irrelevant, professional look.

The parts of Betty, Pearl, Meg, and Surveyor could be played by the same actor.

Act I

ACT I   SCENE 1

The action takes place in the shop.

Grace unlocks the door and enters carrying a full black bin bag. She drops the bag in the middle of the shop then goes through into the storeroom and out of sight.

There are bangs and crashes at the entrance before Clarissa enters shortly after.

CLARISSA   Grace. Grace. (calling) Where are you? You've done it again, haven't you.

Grace enters from the darkened storeroom.

GRACE   Done what?

CLARISSA   You know what. It's the manager's job to open up.

GRACE   I'm not waiting outside for you when I've got my own key.

CLARISSA   You know I'm the registered keyholder. You shouldn't have keys anyway, then there wouldn't be any confusion.

GRACE   I'm not confused. I've been opening up for years. I'll keep them just in case.

CLARISSA	But it's not just in case. It's every blooming day. I'm going to have to speak to Benedict about this.
GRACE	It was Benedict that gave them to me. But that was before your time.
CLARISSA	Never mind about that now; I need you to help me carry something.
GRACE	I'm not supposed to do heavy lifting.
CLARISSA	It's not heavy, it's just awkward.

Clarissa leads Grace off stage. They return, Grace first, carrying a mannequin between them. Grace speaks first before Clarissa is through the door.

GRACE	Blimey, where did you get this thing?
CLARISSA	eBay, it was quite cheap.

They stand the mannequin inside the doorway.

GRACE	You can't leave it there, what are you going to do with it?
CLARISSA	I got it to display the Vintage Range. We'll put it in the window next to the rail.

As they carry mannequin into position.

GRACE	Has she got a name?

CLARISSA She needs a vintage name to promote my vintage range.

GRACE Florence, yet another dummy joins the staff.

The shop door opens and the bell clangs as Ruth enters.

GRACE Speaking of which, here's Ruth.

RUTH Morning, I don't suppose anyone's made the tea.

GRACE I was just going to do it, but Clarissa had me carrying this thing in. Ruth, meet Florence.

RUTH Oh that's nice. At least she won't drink much tea. I'll pop the kettle on.

GRACE Before you do that, do you want to take a look at last night's drop off?

Grace points at the black bag on the floor.

RUTH Okay.

CLARISSA Was it in the doorway again? I wish people wouldn't do that.

RUTH They're donations, Clarissa. We need them.

CLARISSA I've said this before. Bags in the doorway create a bad image. And

	they attract vagrants and vermin. Grace, will you help Ruth sort that bag out?
GRACE	I'm busy doing the float. You can manage can't you Ruth?

Ruth unties the bag during the above and peers inside.

RUTH	Some of it looks a bit tired. Goodness, I hope it's not all like this.

Ruth pulls a thong from the bag and dangles it at arm's length between finger and thumb. Grace bursts out laughing while Clarissa wears a prudish frown.

CLARISSA	That's disgusting. No one would wear those.
GRACE	You're being a prude. Somebody wears them. But I wouldn't buy them second hand.
RUTH	Is that because you don't know where they've been?
GRACE	It's because I know exactly where they've been. Put them in the rag bag along with any other rubbish in there.
RUTH	I'll sort through it first. I don't like throwing anything away, but you could be right about these.

Ruth gives the thong a final shake before returning it to

the bag.

CLARISSA See if there's anything suitable for my Vintage rail.

RUTH There's always old stuff in these bags.

GRACE Ruth, we say vintage now, not old.

RUTH But it's all old, that's why we're given it.

CLARISSA You both know what I mean, and you should stop making fun of my Vintage initiative. I'm trying to attract a different demographic with this strategy.

GRACE Strategy! Demographic! You sound like you've been on a course.

CLARISSA I'm only applying my extensive experience in the retail industry. We need to do something. How much did we take yesterday, Grace?

GRACE Twelve pounds fifty.

CLARISSA It's not enough. That's why I'm developing the Vintage range, and why I bought Florence. When that's established we'll call the bric-a-brac 'Re-purposed and Retro'.

GRACE	Is the kettle on yet, Ruth?
RUTH	I'll do it now while I sort this bag.

Ruth exits to storeroom carrying the bin bag.

GRACE	Why isn't £12.50 enough?
CLARISSA	Because we're losing money.

Door opens, bell rings in comes a customer, Betty.

GRACE	Hello Betty. You escaping Brian again?
BETTY:	Yes. He's a right miserable old sod, does nothing all day.
GRACE	I'm stuck with one just like him. Spends all day in front of the Telly.
BETTY	They'd rather watch rubbish than talk.
GRACE	I know, I only ever get three words from Dennis, 'What's for Dinner'.
BETTY	I've just popped in to look at your books. I'm looking for a good romance. It's the only time I get any.
GRACE	We haven't any new ones since last time you were here. Just more copies of that Fifty Shades thing. You enjoyed that, didn't you?

BETTY I don't know what you're talking about. If you haven't got anything I'll go to Oxfam, they've always got some.

Exit Betty

CLARISSA Why did you have to embarrass her? She left without buying anything. No wonder we're losing money.

GRACE But we all work for nothing. We even buy our own tea.

CLARISSA We've still got the overheads to cover. There's the electric, the insurance, and the rent.

GRACE We don't pay any of that; head office deals with it.

CLARISSA It still has to be paid. If we don't make more than our costs then the charity gets nothing.

GRACE So how much are these costs?

CLARISSA Oh! That's Benedict's department. He's coming today, I had a message from him.

GRACE You know why he's coming and it's not to see us. He'll just pop his head round for five minutes and bugger

	off to see that woman. This is just somewhere to park his car.
CLARISSA	You're just a malicious gossip. You say this every time but never say who she is.
GRACE	I know better than to name names. Why else would he leave his car here for hours? Like most men his brains are below his waist.
CLARISSA	That's unfair. Benedict works very hard for the charity. He has lots of shops to visit, not just us.
GRACE	Benedict works very hard for Benedict. I bet he visits the other shops for the same reason he comes here. A woman for every shop. I wonder who'll arrive first, him or the thief.
CLARISSA	She's not a thief, and she's got a name.
GRACE	Of course she's a thief, that's why she was sent here, to serve her time.
CLARISSA	This isn't a sentence, it's a learning opportunity.
GRACE	You mean we're babysitting because the prisons are full.

CLARISSA	Stephanie has been given a Community Service Order and she'll be working here for twenty hours a week...
GRACE	Working! Ha.
CLARISSA	And while she's here we'll help her learn about retail so she can get a proper job. I expect you and Ruth to help with Stephanie's development.

Ruth comes in carrying two mugs of teas.

RUTH	Young Stephanie? Poor girl, she's a bit of a mess.
GRACE	She's always a mess. You can't do shop work wearing a hoodie and Doc Marten's.
RUTH	That's how young people dress these days. She's probably a goth.
GRACE	Probably a sloth, anyway, she should have been here ten minutes ago. You need to sort her out, Clarissa. She's putting the customers off.
CLARISSA	I'll talk to her about dress protocol when I draw up her development plan.

RUTH   Don't be too hard on her Clarissa, she's not as tough as she pretends to be.

Exit Ruth to stockroom.

GRACE   Be as hard as you like, she needs sorting out.

Stephanie enters through the translucent door. Her hands are deep in her hoodie pockets.

                      Late again.

STEPHANIE   Bus was late.

GRACE   You've only been here a week and you've been late every day.

STEPHANIE   Don't bollock me, bollock the bus.

CLARISSA   Stephanie, I've asked you before, please don't use such foul language. And you mustn't be late every day, you know.

STEPHANIE   What difference does it make?

GRACE   Just shows us what you are, swearing, coming in late, dressing like a...

CLARISSA   (interrupting) Grace, I'm dealing with this.

Steph looks away.

	Stephanie, in this shop you're part of our team and you're here to learn from us.
STEPHANIE	I'm here because I got caught shoplifting. This is punishment.
CLARISSA	No, no, no. This is an opportunity for you, and I'll be writing a report about your progress. I'm sure you'll enjoy working here.
STEPHANIE	Enjoy? All I do is sort rubbish.
CLARISSA:	It's not rubbish. Some of the items we're given are really good quality. We put those on the vintage rail.
STEPHANIE	It comes in bin bags. It's rubbish.
CLARISSA:	You're not helping. I need positive things to put in my report.

Stephanie shrugs

	I know, you need a development plan. We could write it together. We'll include skills like stock control, customer relations, marketing.
GRACE	You could start with punctuality.
CLARISSA	Grace, please.

CLARISSA	I think we should start with stock work. You can help Ruth by sorting the men's from the ladies' clothing and then sort them into sizes.
GRACE	She needs to sort her own clothes out first.
CLARISSA	Grace, stop it. It would help if you wore something a little bit smarter.
STEPHANIE	This is all I've got.

Ruth pokes her head around the stockroom door.

RUTH	Young Stephanie, I thought I heard you. There's a cup of tea in here for you.

Stephanie goes into stock room with Ruth.

GRACE	Well that was a waste of time.
CLARISSA	It's a start. Give her a chance.
GRACE	Get rid of her. Who agreed to her coming anyway?
CLARISSA	Benedict. It might be difficult, but we must do our best for her.
GRACE	But she's so bloody morose.
CLARISSA	Maybe she's just anxious.

Clarissa's phone pings a text message

CLARISSA It's Benedict. He's been delayed by urgent business.

Ruth and Stephanie enter as Clarissa speaks. Stephanie carrying some clothes.

RUTH Well that's strange, because his car's outside.

CLARISSA It can't be, he would've called in.

RUTH It's parked next to yours.

GRACE So he's here, but he's not here. You know where he'll be for the next three hours, don't you.

CLARISSA He can't be long, he's got something important to tell us.

GRACE He hasn't come to see us. He's just come to cook his sausage.

Stephanie laughs.

GRACE What are you laughing at?

STEPHANIE You. Talking about sex.

GRACE Why is that funny? Everybody talks about sex. Some of us have even done it once or twice.

CLARISSA	You shouldn't talk about Benedict like that. He's a married man and he's our manager. He deserves our respect.
RUTH	My George always wanted to, you know, but the drugs affected him. Oh, I remember, we always used to cuddle. I liked the warmth of him snuggling up close. Not all men want the same thing, Grace.
CLARISSA	Has Grace upset you, Ruth?
RUTH	We always said goodnight and kissed. He said it in hospital just before he died. I kissed him and he was gone. I still say goodnight to him every night.
CLARISSA	Perhaps you need to have a break. Maybe you should go and sit in the stock room for a while.
RUTH	I enjoy my memories of George, they keep him alive for me.
CLARISSA	But we have to get ready for Benedict.
GRACE	Can't have emotions in front of Benedict, you'll have to keep your memories to yourself.
RUTH	I like talking about George, we had

	some good times together. You'll have memories one day too, Stephanie.
STEPHANIE	I've got memories.
CLARISSA	Look, we're all getting a little bit upset.
GRACE	Are we?
CLARISSA	We don't have time for this, Benedict will be here soon. Right, Grace, you draw up a list of this month's takings, Ruth, you go and sort out this morning's donations, and I'll pick out some vintage pieces for Florence.
STEPHANIE	What am I supposed to do?
CLARISSA	Oh, you go and help Ruth in the stockroom.

Stephanie goes to stockroom with Ruth.

CLARISSA	How are the takings looking, Grace?
GRACE	Benedict isn't interested. He'll stick his nose in for five minutes, talk to you, ignore us, and clear off.
CLARISSA	He'll want to know about turnover. He'll probably want to speak to Stephanie as well to see how she's

settling in.

GRACE That's easy, she isn't.

CLARISSA Benedict says we can help her, and I agree.

GRACE Benedict doesn't care what we do.

CLARISSA How do you know? Whatever he's planning he wouldn't tell you; you're not the manager.

GRACE I know I'm not the manager; you tell me every day. I bet he never tells you anything anyway.

CLARISSA That's not so. He tells me what goes on in the charity and I tell him what goes on in the shop.

GRACE So you grass on us to Benedict, and he tells you what exactly?

CLARISSA He told me he's coming today to talk about the renewal of our lease.

GRACE What is there to talk about? Nobody else will want this place. The high street is already full of charity shops and estate agents.

CLARISSA It's not that bad. There are the coffee shops, and the bakers.

GRACE   And little else. This town is just a dormitory where retirement dreams turn to nightmares.

Clarissa's phone pings at them to interrupt their convo. She looks at the message, puts her hand to her mouth as she scrolls. Her expression changes.

CLARISSA   It's Benedict. I've got to tell you something.

GRACE   Well what are you waiting for?

CLARISSA   Ruth needs to hear this. And Stephanie. Everyone needs to hear this.

GRACE   He's not resigned has he?

CLARISSA   It's nothing like that. Just for once can you cooperate and go and get Ruth and Stephanie.

GRACE   Okay, okay. I'm doing it.

Grace takes her time going to the stockroom door. When she arrives she opens the door and speaks through it.

Oi, you two, 'the manager' wants to talk to you; she wants you in here, she's had a message.

RUTH   (From inside the storeroom, still unlit) Shall I make some tea?

GRACE	(Relaying to Clarissa) Ruth says shall she make tea?
CLARISSA	(Almost shouting) Oh for God's sake can you just come in here.
GRACE	(Through the door to Ruth) Clarissa says tea will not be required.
RUTH	What?
GRACE	No tea, just come in here.

Ruth and Stephanie emerge from the storeroom into the shop and gather around Clarissa.

CLARISSA	I've had a message from Benedict.
RUTH	I expect he's going to be late again.
CLARISSA	He's told me that the shop is going to close.

Stunned silence.

GRACE	Did you say he's going to close the shop? He can't do that.
CLARISSA	I'm sure it's not Benedict. The owners must want it back.
GRACE	I never did trust him, the bastard.
CLARISSA	Grace, it's not Benedict. The message says 'the charity' so it must

be head office.

RUTH It's a bit sudden. Does he say when?

CLARISSA This is what he says. "The charity has been unable to reach agreement on a new lease. Therefore the shop will close when the lease ends."

GRACE That could be ages, years even.

CLARISSA He's coming today to tell us about it. Where are you going, Stephanie?

STEPHANIE This has nothing to do with me. I'm going to sit in the stockroom. On my own.

Stephanie stomps through the stockroom door, slamming it behind her.

RUTH Is she alright? She looks a bit upset.

GRACE She'll be fine. Makes no difference to her, she's just a crook.

CLARISSA She's not a crook, she's just a youngster who's struggling. I'm going to make sure she's alright.

Clarissa goes to the storeroom.

GRACE I'm not sure what's going on here, Ruth.

RUTH	It looks like the shop's going to close. We'll have to find something else to do.
GRACE	It says at the end of the lease. It could go on for years.
RUTH	Why tell us now if it's not going to happen soon. That other shop closed a couple of years ago.
GRACE	That was the Hamster Society shop. It was failing for ages, no one ever went in there.

Ruth looks around the shop, devoid of customers.

GRACE It's all Benedict's fault.

Clarissa returns from the storeroom alone.

CLARISSA	What's Benedict's fault?
GRACE	The shop closing. He's useless.
RUTH	Is Stephanie alright?
CLARISSA	I don't know. She won't talk to me.
RUTH	I'll go.

Ruth goes to the storeroom.

GRACE So when does this lease expire?

CLARISSA	I honestly don't know.
GRACE	It could have years left.
CLARISSA	That's all dealt with by head office.
GRACE	So our manager has no idea when we get dumped on the street. That's pathetic.
CLARISSA	Benedict will tell us when he gets here.

ACT I   SCENE 2

Lights go down in the shop and up in the storeroom where Stephanie is reading. Enter Ruth.

RUTH I'm making tea, would you like some?

Stephanie, who turned to look when Ruth came in, turns away and rubs a sleeve across her eyes.

Don't be upset, pet. There'll be other places you can go.

STEPHANIE: Uh?

RUTH If the shop closes. There's no need to get upset about it. Like you say, it's only a charity shop.

STEPHANIE I couldn't care less about the fucking shop.

RUTH There's no need to swear. Whatever's the matter, pet.

STEPHANIE Nothing. And don't call me pet. I'm not your little furry animal.

RUTH Sorry, Stephanie. I just thought you looked a bit tearful.

Stephanie shoves her book into the pocket of her jeans. She tries to do this without being noticed, but Ruth sees her.

	Ah, you've been reading. Books can be very emotional can't they. That's why I don't read thrillers, they keep me awake. Is it a sad story you're reading?
STEPHANIE	No.
RUTH	Is it one of those magic books? They're all the rage with young people these days aren't they?
STEPHANIE	If you mean Harry Potter, that's for kids. And if you must know I'm reading poetry.
RUTH	That's interesting. Have you read any Pam Ayres? She always makes me laugh.
STEPHANIE	No.
RUTH	You should try her. Sometimes she's on the Radio, but I don't suppose you listen to that?
STEPHANIE	No.
RUTH	What sort of poems do you like reading then?
STEPHANIE	Why do you want to know?

RUTH	I'm just chatting while I make the tea. You know, sharing stuff. It's what people do when they work together.
STEPHANIE	Do they?
RUTH	I expect you've done it yourself when you've been at work.
STEPHANIE	I've never had a job.
RUTH	Well you're here now, and it's what we do when we work together, we chat. It makes the day go by quicker. Now tell me about this poetry book of yours. Is it from our shop?
STEPHANIE:	No. My granddad gave it to me.
RUTH	Who's it by?
STEPHANIE	It's an anthology. It's by lots of people.
RUTH	That's nice. You'll get lots of different poets in there. Have you got a favourite.
STEPHANIE	I like "The Road not Taken", do you know it?
RUTH	I think I might have heard of it. Is it jolly.

STEPHANIE	No.
RUTH	Anything cheerful will do for me. My George said, before he died. "Don't you go getting all miserable, you get on with your life." He was good was George. And I did, I got on with things. That's why I'm here, doing good instead of moping about at home. But I do miss him. And home feels awfully empty when I get there. And do you know, sometimes I call out his name, but of course there's no answer.
STEPHANIE	Do you have to go on about bloody George. I don't want to hear about him.
RUTH	There's no need for that. George was my husband for nearly forty years, before the cancer killed him. I can't help it if I miss him. You should make allowances for people.
STEPHANIE	Why. People don't make allowances for me.
RUTH	It takes a while to get over losing someone you've known nearly all your life. You'll learn that as you get older. It leaves a great big hole that's really difficult to fill. But then it's not as if you've lost anyone.

STEPHANIE   I thought you were making tea.

Ruth finishes making the tea in silence, back to Steph, clearly upset. She plonks a mug down near Steph.

RUTH   Here's your tea.

She picks up three mugs on a tray and heads for the door, as she gets there:

STEPHANIE   Wait a minute.

Ruth pauses and turns to face Steph.

RUTH   What.

STEPHANIE   Nothing. Thanks for the tea.

Ruth leaves the storeroom and the lights go down there, coming up in the shop as she enters.

ACT I SCENE 3

Ruth enters the shop from the storeroom carrying a tray with three mugs. Not much has changed.

CLARISSA Oh, good. Tea.

Ruth sets the tray down by the till. As Grace takes a mug she says:

GRACE At last, what have you been doing, growing it?

Ruth looks a little confused and Grace explains:

It's a joke, Ruth. You used to be a bit quicker on the uptake. Oh, and it's Wednesday today, in case you need reminding.

Ruth's confusion grows.

RUTH I don't understand what you mean.

GRACE These are the first signs. It's definitely happening, Clarissa.

RUTH Whatever are you on about?

CLARISSA Take no notice of her, she's in one of her moods this morning.

GRACE It's the first signs, confusion, loss of sense of humour, not knowing what

	day it is. You're losing it Ruth. You'll be coming in with your clothes inside out by next week. Then you'll be forgetting to...
CLARISSA	Stop it Grace, you're being cruel.

Ruth checks her clothes and looks pleadingly at Clarissa.

RUTH	I feel just the same as I did yesterday. I'm not getting forgetful, am I?
CLARISSA	Of course you're not. No more than the rest of us. Mind you, you were quite a long time with the tea.
GRACE	Loss of a sense of time, that's another symptom.
CLARISSA	Do stop it, Grace.
RUTH	I was with Stephanie, but she's not easy to talk to.
GRACE	Try talking to her about shoplifting, she knows about that.
CLARISSA	Young people do have difficulty communicating these days. I'll put communication skills in her development plan.
GRACE	What's the point of that if we're going to be shut down and kicked

	out. How's your "Development Plan" going to work on the street?
CLARISSA	But we don't know when that's going to happen. You said it could be ages before the lease runs out. Young Stephanie could have completed her Community Service by then.
GRACE	You're ignoring the tea leaves, Clarissa. Why has Benedict told us now? If it's years before it closes we might be in a better place.
RUTH	Do you mean the food bank? I'd like that.
GRACE	No Ruth, not the food bank. I mean we could all be dead.

Enter Customer 2 - Pearl, wheeling a suitcase.

GRACE	You going away again Pearl?
PEARL:	Yes, I've brought you last year's holiday clothes.
CLARISSA	Where are you off to this time?
PEARL	Benidorm, again. I want to go to Barcelona, but Ted likes Benidorm.
CLARISSA	I loved Barcelona, mind you that was twenty years ago now.

PEARL	Ted says it's too expensive. Have you been Grace?
GRACE	We don't go anywhere.
PEARL	You should, you could do with some sun. Might cheer you up a bit. Can you empty the case for me please, I need it.
RUTH:	I'm not sure there's enough room for it just now. Can you bring it back later?
PEARL	No, I need to go home and pack. If you can't have it, I'll take it to Oxfam.

Exit Pearl with case.

GRACE	She only comes here because we're nearest, showing off as usual.
CLARISSA	There might have been something in there suitable for my Vintage range.
RUTH	I doubt it, her donations are never the best. What will we do with all this stock when the shop closes?
CLARISSA	Don't be so negative. We don't know for sure if it's actually going to happen. We'll just have to wait to talk to Benedict.

GRACE You can't trust him, he's a scheming bastard.

CLARISSA He's not a scheming... I'm sure he doesn't want to close the shop any more than you. Why would he?

GRACE He'll say we don't take enough money. But really he's doing it to impress his boss. He doesn't care about us.

CLARISSA Nonsense. When he gets here we'll know. He likes my vintage idea, so I'm sure he'll want to keep the shop open.

GRACE I don't trust him, and nor should you. He's cheating on his wife and he's cheating on us.

CLARISSA How can you say that about Benedict?

GRACE Why not? It's the truth. He's threatening to close our shop and you're the manager, what are you doing about it?

CLARISSA I'm doing everything I can. But we all need to pull together, with Benedict, if we're going to keep the shop open.

GRACE He's screwing everyone, including

	us. You should contact his bosses, tell them what he's doing.
CLARISSA	Now you are being silly. I'm sure he's only following instructions.
GRACE	Then why isn't he here to tell us himself? This is just somewhere to park his car.
RUTH	He's got to leave it somewhere.
GRACE	He cares more about his car than he does about the shop. Well his car might develop some faults before he gets back.
RUTH	You should count to ten before you do anything in anger Grace.
GRACE	I'm not angry. I'm bloody furious.
RUTH	My George always said there's no point in getting angry, you've just got to learn to live with it.
GRACE	Live with what for Christ's sake? Council tax?
RUTH	Cancer.
CLARISSA	You've gone too far again Grace. You always go too far.
RUTH	It's alright. George has gone now.

                    The cancer's over, his suffering's
                    over; you can't upset me anymore.

GRACE   Not bloody George again.

Grace exits to storeroom

ACT I	**SCENE 4**
GRACE	What are you doing here?
STEPHANIE	What d'you mean? Why am I here sorting through other people's rubbish? Fuck knows.
GRACE	Why are you in this grubby charity shop with three old women?
STEPHANIE	I got caught shoplifting and got sent here. Why are you in a grubby charity shop.
GRACE	I don't have to explain myself to you.
STEPHANIE	What are you asking me for then?
GRACE	Because this is my shop and you shouldn't be here.
STEPHANIE	It's not your effing shop. Haven't you heard? They're throwing you out.
GRACE	I knew you'd be trouble the minute I saw you.
STEPHANIE	And I knew you'd be a stuck-up old gimmer. Why don't you piss off and leave me alone.
GRACE	If anyone needs to leave it's you. Do you swear at your parents like this? I

	bet your mum and dad are really proud of you.
STEPHANIE	Yeah, and you've got perfect kids.

A silence for a short time.

GRACE	You just shouldn't be here.
STEPHANIE	Well I am, and I haven't got any choice. Why don't you leave?
GRACE	You're young. You might even be bright under that sullen exterior. Why aren't you making something of your life instead of thieving?
STEPHANIE	I'm supposed to be doing community service. It's a joke; they said there'd be opportunities.
GRACE	We don't need you here. You could just go, no one would care.
STEPHANIE	Clarissa would.
GRACE	Clarissa is so desperate she'll latch on to anyone. Even you.
STEPHANIE	So Clarissa's desperate, Ruth's losing it, and I shouldn't be here. What's wrong with you?
GRACE	There's nothing wrong with me.

STEPHANIE Yes, you're just fucking perfect, aren't you. You've got no idea what my life's like.

GRACE Why would I want to know about you? I've got enough problems of my own.

STEPHANIE What problems have you got?

GRACE I've lost more in my life than you'll ever have.

STEPHANIE Like what?

GRACE Like my son.

STEPHANIE Is he dead?

GRACE He went to Australia. I haven't seen him for twenty years.

STEPHANIE Haven't you been to see him?

GRACE Dennis won't go.

STEPHANIE You could go on your own.

GRACE It's not as simple as that.

STEPHANIE Why not? Can't he come and see you?

GRACE He's got his own wife and kids now. He's not bothered about me.

STEPHANIE	I know how that feels. You were right, no one gives a shit about me.
GRACE	You've got family haven't you? You've got a mum and dad?
STEPHANIE	I've never had a dad. All mum cares about is getting a man, but they never stay.
GRACE	Isn't there anyone else? Aunts, uncles, grandparents?
STEPHANIE	Not anymore. You should go to Australia and see your grandkids.
GRACE	I'm too old now.
STEPHANIE	This place is closing, go and see them.
GRACE	They won't want to see me. I'm a stranger to them.
STEPHANIE	I bet Clarissa thinks you should.
GRACE	Clarissa doesn't care what I do. She's got no one. Husband left years ago; he was a lying bastard just like Benedict. She should have known he'd bugger off. It's all her own fault.
STEPHANIE	What is?
GRACE	Everything that's wrong with her life.

                                                She thinks Benedict listens to her, but he thinks she's just as stupid as the rest of us. Look at what he's doing to the shop.

STEPHANIE   What are you going to do about it?

GRACE   I wish I fucking knew.

Lights down.

ACT I   SCENE 5

Clarissa and Ruth on stage. Clarissa pulls out a flip chart stand.

CLARISSA   We need to draw up an action plan to show Benedict it's worth keeping the shop open.

RUTH   Is that going to work?

CLARISSA   Of course it is. Get Grace and Stephanie in here. We need everyone's input.

Ruth goes to storeroom door.

RUTH   Clarissa says can you both come in, she's had an idea.

Enter Grace and Stephanie.

GRACE   What's the big idea? Not another bloody training day I hope.

CLARISSA   We need to draw up a plan to show Benedict how we'll make the shop viable.

GRACE   What sort of plan?

CLARISSA   Things we can do to increase the turnover, like my vintage idea. If we send him our proposals he can go

	through them with us. We can add other things like moving to another shop or sharing with another charity.
RUTH	Like the food bank? I'd like that.

Door opens, in comes Meg.

GRACE	Hello Meg, haven't seen you for weeks.
MEG:	We've been to my daughters in Manchester, seeing our latest grandson. He's a gorgeous little chap, you'd love him.
RUTH	How lovely.
MEG	I like Manchester, there's so much to do. But I don't suppose you've ever been, have you, Grace?
GRACE	Why would I want to go there. What have you come in for anyway?
MEG	I've brought some photos of little Tobias to show you.

Meg scrolls through her phone.

CLARISSA	He's gorgeous, look at those chubby little cheeks. You're so lucky.
MEG	Here's another photo.

RUTH	That's a lovely little hat.
MEG	I'm glad you noticed the hat. I made it myself. Look Grace.
GRACE	Now we've seen it are you going to buy anything?
MEG	No, you've got nothing I want. I'm just doing the rounds with my photos.
RUTH	Aren't you going to stop for a cup of tea?
MEG	No thanks, I'll have a coffee with the girls in Oxfam.

Exit Meg.

RUTH	Those were lovely pictures.
CLARISSA	He was a bonny little lad wasn't he?
GRACE	Now she's gone can we get back to this plan you were talking about.
CLARISSA	Okay Grace. Let's do some brainstorming. Give me your best ideas.

Clarissa opens up a flip chart and stands poised with a pen.

GRACE	What, like give us our shop back?

CLARISSA No Grace, positive things we can do to keep the shop open.

GRACE Such as?

CLARISSA Well, we've already got the Vintage Range, or moving the shop, our work with young people like Stephanie. How we can attract younger customers.

RUTH What about that re-doing thing you said.

CLARISSA Good Ruth, Re-purposed and Retro, I'd forgotten about that. And Stephanie, have you got any ideas we could use to attract younger people like you?

STEPHANIE What? To buy this shit?

RUTH Are you going to send this to Benedict.

GRACE He won't read it.

CLARISSA (Photographs Flip Chart with phone) I've sent it to him now, so he'll have to talk about it. It's our agenda for the meeting.

GRACE So where is he?

CLARISSA He'll be here soon. He'll help us

	implement it.
GRACE	What does that mean?

Phone pings.

CLARISSA	(LOOKS AT PHONE) He says he likes our proposal but it's too late. The shop closes next week.

End of Act one - Interval

Act II

ACT II   SCENE 1

The characters all adopt the precise position they were in at the end of Act 1. Clarissa is looking at her phone. There is an air of stunned silence.

GRACE Say that again, Clarissa.

CLARISSA He says the shop is closing next week. There's somebody coming to measure up today.

RUTH We've still got time to organise the stock, make sure...

GRACE (interrupting) The bastard. How long has he known about this?

CLARISSA Grace, mind your language.

GRACE He is a bastard, and I won't mind my language. When he gets here I'll ... (PAUSE) He's just a bastard.

Grace struggles to contain her of anger and upset. She turns on her heel and stomps to the door; yanks it open with such force the jangling bell above the door falls off; and slams the door as she leaves. Stephanie bursts out laughing in the stunned silence that ensues.

CLARISSA I don't know what you're laughing at.

STEPHANIE Don't you think it's funny? People

	laugh at me when I get in a strop.
CLARISSA	She shouldn't let her feelings run away with her. It sets a bad example.
STEPHANIE	Who to? Me?
CLARISSA	Exactly. And I was hoping she'd be part of your development plan.
STEPHANIE	Development plan? You are fucking joking. The shop closes next week.
CLARISSA	Stephanie, please don't use that language. The plan will still help you get on in life, get a proper job, earn a living. But Grace isn't helping. She's behaving like a teenager.
STEPHANIE	If that's how teenagers behave, I'll join her.

Stephanie follows in Grace's footsteps, kicking the doorbell aside as she exits.

CLARISSA   What's got into them?

She stoops to recover the now bent doorbell.

Look at this, it's ruined. I'm as upset as Grace, but I'm the manager, I can't walk out.

RUTH   Does it matter if the shop closes. It's

	been fun, but there's plenty of charity work to do.
CLARISSA	The shop hasn't closed yet. We've got until next week. If we can convince Benedict that our plan will work, we might get a reprieve.
RUTH	If you really want to try to keep it open I'll help while I can, but you really need Grace on board as well.
CLARISSA	I don't know. Grace is so grumpy and argumentative.
RUTH	I get on with her.
CLARISSA	You don't have to manage her. Where do you think she's gone?
RUTH	She'll be back when she's cooled down.

The door opens, Ruth and Clarissa look expectant. In walks Stephanie.

CLARISSA	Stephanie, where have you been? Have you seen Grace?
STEPHANIE	Nowhere. Yes.
CLARISSA	D'you know, Sometimes I don't understand a word you say.
RUTH	She says she's been nowhere, and

	yes, she has seen Grace. Is that right Stephanie?
STEPHANIE	Yeah. It's not hard if you listen, is it?
CLARISSA	Where did you see her?
STEPHANIE	She was in the bakers. It looked like she was throwing a right strop in there too.
CLARISSA	What am I going to do with her?
STEPHANIE	She's just being herself. Why do you have to do anything with her?
CLARISSA	Because we've got so much to do if we're going to save the shop.

Enter Grace carrying a box from the bakers.

RUTH	Is that cake?
GRACE	Yes Ruth, these are special doomsday cakes fresh from the bakers down the street. Would you like one?
RUTH	Well, I shouldn't really; but seeing as you've brought them specially. Shall I make some tea?
GRACE	That is your most marvellous idea in all the years you've worked here.

RUTH	Pardon?
GRACE	Yes Ruth, put the kettle on and make more tea.

Ruth goes to the storeroom to make tea.

GRACE	She says she's diabetic, but I've never known her to refuse cake. When she comes back she'll say, 'One won't do any harm'.
CLARISSA	You don't begrudge her this small pleasure do you?
GRACE	Course not. Take your pleasures while you can I say. That's why I've bought cake. A little light relief from this unremitting misery we call life.
CLARISSA	Are you alright, Grace?
GRACE	I'm bloody fantastic. Have a cake.

Grace opens the box to display four cakes, all different. Ruth reappears with a tray of tea mugs.

CLARISSA	May I have the custard slice. Unless anyone else wants it.
GRACE	I had you down for that one, thin skinned and lacking in meaningful substance.

Clarissa loads the cake onto a plate brought by Ruth.

	What about you, Ruth?
RUTH	One won't do any harm. Can I have the Danish, they're my favourite.
GRACE	Of course you can, Ruth. I'm told that amongst the cornucopia of cakes on offer the Danish pastry is not only the most popular, but also contains the most sugar. Stephanie, I think you should have the Chocolate eclair.
STEPHANIE	Why?
GRACE	Because it's dark and rough on the outside, but really very soft in the middle.
STEPHANIE	What's that you're having?
GRACE	This is a Cream horn. Something I've not had for decades.

They all take a bite at the same time. Clarissa's phone rings. Clarissa tries to dash to her desk with cake in one hand and tea in the other. She puts them down and wipes her fingers on a tissue to pick up her phone.

CLARISSA	(through a mouthful of cake) It's Benedict.

As she picks the phone up it stops ringing before she can swipe it.

>   I've missed it. See what you made
>   me do with your stupid cakes.

GRACE   I didn't make you have one. If it's
                         urgent he'll ring back.

Clarissa's phone blips for an incoming text message.

CLARISSA   He's been delayed. He says we're to
                         make the surveyors welcome when
                         they arrive and to clear...

Clarissa becomes tearful. Ruth moves to her.

RUTH   What is it, Clarissa, what's he say.

Clarissa pushes the phone at Ruth.

>   Oh, Benedict says to 'clear the
>   rubbish out of the window so they
>   can measure up.'

GRACE   That'll be your precious 'vintage' rail,
                         and Florence. I told you he doesn't
                         care.

Grace calmly takes a sip of tea and another bite of her cream horn while Clarissa flees to the storeroom and solitude.

RUTH   That was cruel, Grace. There are
                         other things in the window.

GRACE   But it's the rail that'll get in the way
                         when they measure up.

Vintage

RUTH You know how Clarissa feels about her vintage rail. It was just so... unnecessary.

GRACE The truth is never unnecessary, Ruth. Avoid it and you make mistakes. Like ending up here.

STEPHANIE You're wrong. The truth doesn't stop you from making mistakes.

GRACE What do you mean?

RUTH Don't take any notice of her, Stephanie. (To Grace) I'm going to check on Clarissa, and you, leave the girl alone.

Ruth leaves to the storeroom, Grace calls after her...

GRACE She's not a girl she's a... (The door to the storeroom closes and Grace stops).

STEPHANIE I'm a what?

GRACE You're a young woman in trouble. Why did you have to go thieving?

STEPHANIE I needed a dress. What's it to you?

GRACE That's not your style. What did you need it for?

STEPHANIE I needed a black one, to go to a

	funeral.
GRACE	And you got caught.
STEPHANIE	Yeah. I wasn't thinking straight. The shop was too posh, I didn't belong. They were watching me as soon as I walked in.
GRACE	So did you go?
STEPHANIE	Go where?
GRACE	To the funeral. Without the dress.
STEPHANIE	Course I did. But I had to wear my jeans. What do you want to know for?
GRACE	I like to know about the people I work with.
STEPHANIE	This isn't work. The court sent me here just because I needed a dress for a funeral.
GRACE	Why didn't you buy it then?
STEPHANIE	I didn't have any money.
GRACE	Whose funeral was it?
STEPHANIE	It was my Granddad's. He taught me to show respect when someone dies. That's why I wanted a black

dress.

GRACE The dress wasn't for you, then.

Stephanie remains silent.

It must have been hard, losing your Grandad.

STEPHANIE It was horrible. My mum chucked him out and he died in a care home after. He should have stayed with us. I could have been with him.

GRACE What could you have done? You can't stop death. You just have to accept it.

STEPHANIE But if I'd been there I could have said goodbye.

GRACE Death isn't like that. It's not like seeing someone off at the station. There's no romance, just the end of a story. The best bits stay with you. That's what you need to do. Remember the best bits of your granddad.

STEPHANIE But I miss him. He was the only one who cared about me.

GRACE I know what you mean. I love my son, but he's gone to a new life on the other side of the world.

STEPHANIE He isn't dead. He's in Australia. It's not the same.

GRACE He might as well be dead. I never hear from him. But you've got to get on with your life. Grab the opportunities that come your way.

STEPHANIE You sound like Clarissa and her development plan.

GRACE Clarissa makes plans instead of doing things. You don't need a plan.

STEPHANIE She's writing a report about me.

GRACE She'll write a report about her plan, not about you. Take no notice of her.

STEPHANIE I have to, or I'll get into trouble.

GRACE No you won't. Just make something of your life or you'll end up like us lot. Humiliated by a bastard who hasn't even the decency to come and see us. If he closes this shop I want my revenge.

STEPHANIE You sound like a kid in the playground.

GRACE Why shouldn't I? I want to kick him where it hurts, right in his nasty little ego.

Clarissa enters phone in hand.

CLARISSA	Grace, I've had another message from Benedict. He wants to explain the whole situation personally.
GRACE	I don't believe him.
CLARISSA	He says he's very sorry about everything.
GRACE	Why would he tell you that?
CLARISSA	He often tells me what he thinks. I am the manager.

Ruth's phone rings in the stockroom. It stops when answered.

GRACE	That'll be the woman who runs the food bank. Steph, go do a bit of earwigging in the storeroom, find out what Ruth's up to.
STEPHANIE	Why don't you.
GRACE	She'll clam up if I go in there, but she'll take no notice of you. Say you're looking for something for a customer.

Stephanie glances at Clarissa.

STEPHANIE	I'm not staying if she asks me to leave.

GRACE	Of course not but hurry up or she'll be finished.

Stephanie exits to the storeroom.

	(To Clarissa) You needn't look at me like that. You want to know as much as I do.
CLARISSA	It's Ruth's business. It's got nothing to do with us.
GRACE	But you still want Steph to find out. You're such a stuck-up prig.
CLARISSA	There's no need to be so offensive. I just wonder why she'd be speaking to the foodbank.
GRACE	I'll spell it out for you, shall I. Ruth thinks we're closing, the food bank needs people, and she's going to volunteer.
CLARISSA	Ruth can't go to the food bank. We need her here.
GRACE	Not for much longer if Benedict the Bastard has his way.
CLARISSA	Why must you turn everything into something nasty. It puts people off.
GRACE	Why should I care what people think? They never care about me.

	And everything is nasty. Benedict is nasty, this shop is nasty, the people who come in here are nasty.
CLARISSA	But you're in a customer facing role. How can we be successful with attitudes like that. Sometimes you make me so cross.
GRACE	"Customer Facing", my God, you are so up yourself, Clarissa. We don't have customers; we have either the desperate or the tight-fisted. And it's not me making you angry, you're doing that.
CLARISSA	It is you with your constant complaining and unwillingness to learn. I've tried to teach you about retail, goodness knows I have. But you take no notice.
GRACE	Help me with retail! Just once get off that pedestal and see things as they really are.
CLARISSA	You won't talk to the customers properly, you won't help Ruth with the sorting. And now you won't even help poor young Stephanie.
GRACE	I'll have you know "poor young Stephanie" and I actually get along fine. And if you stopped treating her like a project you might get on with

her as well.

CLARISSA I don't see any evidence of you getting on with her. You're always on at that poor girl. At least I'm doing something for her with my development plan.

GRACE That's what I mean. Your development plan, nothing to do with Steph. If it makes you feel good, that's fine. It doesn't matter if it's no use to her.

Clarissa opens her mouth to reply but cannot. She turns away from Grace. Silence.

CLARISSA They've been in there a long time. I'm going to see what's happening.

Clarissa heads for the storeroom door, hiding her face from Grace. As she approaches the door opens and Steph comes into the shop. Clarissa exits into the storeroom.

ACT II **SCENE 2**

The lights go down on the shop and up on the storeroom. Ruth is sitting on a stool as Clarissa enters.

RUTH	Are you alright, Clarissa?
CLARISSA	(fanning herself with a hand) Yes, yes. I'm fine.
RUTH	You don't look fine. You look as though you've been crying.
CLARISSA	No, no. I, I... (she breaks down in tears).
RUTH	Whatever's the matter? Shall I make some tea?
CLARISSA	(Through her tears) I don't want any more of your bloody tea, I'm swimming in the stuff.
RUTH	I'm only trying to help.
CLARISSA	(regaining control) I'm sorry, Ruth. I don't think if I can stand it any longer.
RUTH	Has Grace been upsetting you again.
CLARISSA	I don't understand why she has to be so horrid all the time.

RUTH   She's not a very happy person.

CLARISSA   She never has a good word to say about anything. Especially me, or the shop.

RUTH   I expect she has her own troubles.

CLARISSA   We all have troubles, not just her. I've got problems of my own. I'm here every day, making sure the shop runs smoothly. What do I get? Grace's bad temper.

RUTH   We all come and do our best every day.

CLARISSA   You don't have to manage her. She's ruining this shop.

RUTH   It's not Grace that's closing the shop. It means a lot to her.

CLARISSA   Then she should behave as though it does.

RUTH   She's been here a long time, and she turns up every day.

CLARISSA   I've put so much into this place.

RUTH   There'll be another opportunity for you, but Grace might struggle.

CLARISSA   No there won't. There isn't anything

else.

RUTH Something will turn up.

CLARISSA Without this shop I'll be on my own and have nothing to do.

RUTH Neither will Grace. But you must have friends.

CLARISSA Not now. I did, before Jack left. But when he went I lost them. I tried to keep in touch, but they were always busy.

RUTH People are busy these days. Don't you ever see your family?

CLARISSA There is only me. We never had any children. And I'm an only child. The only friends I have are in this shop and now it might close. What am I going to do?

RUTH I don't know.

CLARISSA It doesn't seem to bother you, that the shop might close.

RUTH Well there's always something needs doing somewhere. I'm going to work in the food bank. Dorothy asked me when I can start. I told her it will be in a week or so.

CLARISSA What about me?

RUTH I don't think they need a manager.

ACT II   SCENE 3

Lights go down on storeroom, lights go up on shop area. Stephanie and Grace on stage.

STEPHANIE Is this all you three ever do, argue with each other?

GRACE That's not true. I never argue with Ruth.

STEPHANIE But you're always taking the piss out of her. You don't argue with her because she won't bite back. Fuck knows why she's here.

GRACE She's here because she needs the company, just like the rest of us. It gets her out of the house.

STEPHANIE So it's okay for Ruth to be here, and Clarissa, and you. But you want rid of me.

GRACE Why would you want to be here? You should be at home.

STEPHANIE Home's crap.

GRACE Home should be a good place for you.

STEPHANIE Well it isn't. Mum says I'm sponging off her. She doesn't like me, and she

	wants me out.
GRACE	Where will you go?
STEPHANIE	There isn't anywhere.
GRACE	There must be places to help young people like you.
STEPHANIE	There's nowhere. It's all about money and I haven't got any.
GRACE	Well you know how to get money don't you?
STEPHANIE	What? You mean steal it?
GRACE:	No, I mean work for it, get a job.
STEPHANIE	There aren't any, no one would have me anyway.
GRACE	You could get a job. You're bright enough. You've just got to behave like somebody who wants one.
STEPHANIE	That's what you say, what do you know about it.
GRACE	I'm just trying to help. Just like your granddad would.
STEPHANIE	You're not my granddad.

Enter surveyor.

SURV:	Hello, I'm looking for Clarissa. Would that be you?
GRACE	Why? What do you want?
SURV	I need to speak to the manager and I believe that's her name.
GRACE	(Shouts) Clarissa, someone wants to speak to the manager.

Clarissa enters the shop.

CLARISSSA	I'm the manager. What can I do for you?
SURV	Good morning. I'm from the landlord's office. We need to do a survey before we take the shop back. I'm here to fix a date.
GRACE	In about ten years.
SURV	Mr Beckett suggested this week.
GRACE	Did Benedict the Bastard send you?
CLARISSA	I'm ever so sorry, we're all a bit upset. We've only just been told that the shop is closing. We thought the lease would be renewed.
SURV	So did we.
GRACE	Did you say you thought the lease

	was going to be renewed?
SURV	Well there's absolutely no market for retail space. Charity shops like this work for us right now.
CLARISSA	So why didn't you agree a new lease?
SURV	We offered. Mr Beckett said it was no longer required.
GRACE	He's been lying to us all the time. He's only closing the shop because he wants to.
CLARISSA	We don't know that. He might have another property in mind for us.
GRACE	Get him here Clarissa. He needs to explain himself.
SURV	Look I really didn't mean to start anything. These are my details (HANDS OVER CARD). Please call me when you have a convenient date for the survey. Thank you.

Exit surveyor.

GRACE	Where is he Clarissa? Where is that bastard?
CLARISSA	He'll be here soon. We know he's got to come back to collect his car.

GRACE This is your fault for trusting him.

CLARISSA Let's not blame each other. We've all got to work together to save the shop.

GRACE We are. He's not. You're the manager. Get him here.

CLARISSA I'm just a volunteer, like you. I have to do what he says. I only know he's coming because he told me.

Ruth enters the shop.

RUTH Are you talking about Benedict? Well his car's gone. It doesn't look like he's coming.

GRACE What did you say?

STEPHANIE She said his car's gone. He's done a runner.

CLARISSA He can't have gone. Let me look.

Clarissa exits into the stockroom to check for herself.

GRACE This isn't a joke, is it?

RUTH No, he's definitely gone.

CLARISSA (Rushing back in) She's right, his car's gone. He must have gone to get some petrol, or something. I'm

	sure he'll be back.
GRACE	Face it Clarissa. He's done the dirty on us and buggered off.
CLARISSA	I don't understand, he's always tried his best for us and the shop.
GRACE	He's always tried his best for himself. He's taken us all for granted. It's all my life has ever been.
CLARISSA	I don't take you for granted.
GRACE	You do it all the time. "Grace, do the takings, Grace help Ruth, Grace look after Stephanie".
STEPHANIE	I know how it feels.
GRACE	And don't you start... What did you say?
STEPHANIE	I know how it feels, being taken for granted. My mum does it all the time. She's always on at me. I have to do everything she says. Cooking and cleaning and looking after little Jason. Even then I'm always in the way.
CLARISSA	Oh she's your mum, I'm sure she loves you.
STEPHANIE	She doesn't love me. No one does.

Steph begins to sob and dashes off to the storeroom.

CLARISSA She's really upset. What have we done?

GRACE This is your fault, Clarissa, not mine. You blame me for everything. It's my fault we don't have enough customers, it's my fault the shop's closing down. It's probably my fault that Jack left you, although I can see why he did.

CLARISSA Now you're being cruel as well as selfish and I won't listen to it. I'm going to calm the poor girl down.

GRACE No you're not. She doesn't need your bleeding development plans; she needs someone who understands her. I'll go.

Grace exits to the storeroom.

ACT II SCENE 4

Grace exits to the storeroom Lights down on shop, up on storeroom.

STEPHANIE	What have you come in for, come to take the piss because you've made me cry?
GRACE	No, love. There's nothing to gloat about when someone's upset.
STEPHANIE	So what have you come in for then.
GRACE	I'm here to help you love.
STEPHANIE	There's nothing you can do. And don't call me "love". I'm not your love and you're not mine.
GRACE	I would call you by your name but I'm never sure if you prefer Steph or Stephanie.
STEPHANIE	(lifting her head a little) I prefer Steph. My mum calls me Stephanie.
GRACE	Alright Steph. You may think I don't understand, but I had a rotten time as a teenager as well.
STEPHANIE	Oh yeah? I bet you had a dad though.

GRACE	Oh yes. You're right, I did have a dad. That was the problem.
STEPHANIE	He didn't... you know...
GRACE	No, he never did anything like that. In some ways it was worse.
STEPHANIE	What could be worse than that?

Lights down on storeroom, up on shop

Clarissa and Ruth still on stage.

CLARISSA	Why is Grace so horrid all the time?
RUTH	I don't think she means to be. She's just doing the best she can. Pretty much like you and me, really.
CLARISSA	She does the best she can to irritate me. She never cooperates, she's forever complaining, and now, when we need to pull together, she's offensive.
RUTH	She has got a point about Benedict though. He's never been supportive of this shop. His visits are always short. He never tells us anything. We only ever get snippets of the messages he sends. Has he told you much about what's going on?
CLARISSA	If I tell you something will you not

	tell Grace?
RUTH	I don't like secrets, not in the workplace. But if it will help you then tell me, I won't let on to Grace.
CLARISSA	Benedict tells me hardly anything. He doesn't recognise all my hard work, and just uses me to pass messages on to everybody. He hasn't told me where he is today, and now he's gone. I just don't know what to do. The surveyor says Benedict could have renewed the lease, but I didn't know. It's horrible how he's treated me.
RUTH	You should tell him how you feel.
CLARISSA	How can I? I never see him on my own, it's always in our meetings. And I can't tell him over the phone. If he answers, he always has something important to do and fobs me off.
RUTH	Maybe you should forget about Benedict. Go and work somewhere else.
CLARISSA	I like it here, I've got responsibilities. If I go somewhere else I won't know anyone. I'll be starting at the bottom.
RUTH	Well, we are all volunteers.

CLARISSA	But what do you think would people make of me?
RUTH	I find if you get on with your job most people are friendly and they'll like you.
CLARISSA	That might be easy for you, but people don't like me.

Lights down on shop and up on storeroom

GRACE	I was about your age when I met Dennis. He was a bit older than me. I fell in love with him and of course I got pregnant.
STEPHANIE	What's that got to do with your dad if it was Dennis who got you pregnant?
GRACE	We weren't married then. And when my dad found out, he chucked me out of the house. Said I should have had the sense to keep my legs closed. Those were his exact words.
STEPHANIE	What did you do?
GRACE	I went and told Dennis I was expecting, and he said we should get married. I didn't know what I was doing really, but only my mum came to the wedding. Then after we were married, I lost the baby.

STEPHANIE	That's terrible.
GRACE	It was. And a few months later I got pregnant again. I was so worried it would happen again. Dennis didn't understand. Men don't.
STEPHANIE	Then what happened?
GRACE	I had a baby, didn't I. Your life changes when you have a baby. You don't care about anything else as long as your child is alright.
STEPHANIE	My mum never cared what happened to me. I was always too gobby, or too greedy, or in the way.
GRACE	Thing is, you don't get taught how to be a mum, you have to learn it on the job. Perhaps your grandmother was horrible to your mother and that's all she knows about what mums do.
STEPHANIE	That and shagging every bloke she meets. Some of them are right losers.
GRACE	None of them try it on with you, do they?
STEPHANIE	No, I've had to scream at one or two, but that's all. So what happened after you had your baby?

GRACE He was just so beautiful. I fell in love with him straight away. I knew, right from when I first held him, that I'd do anything to keep him safe, to give him what he needed. I've never felt anything so powerful.

STEPHANIE So it all turned out okay for you and Dennis?

GRACE God no. Dennis was useless. I soon fell out of love with him. I would have left but I didn't want Tom to grow up without his dad. I just put up with Dennis.

STEPHANIE But you're still with him now.

GRACE You get into habits, fixed ways. That's why I come here every day.

STEPHANIE My mum never talks to me like this.

GRACE No, nor did mine. Come on, let's take them in some tea.

STEPHANIE Okay.

ACT II   SCENE 5

Shop, Grace and Stephanie enter carrying tea.

GRACE	Here you are, wc've made you some tea.
RUTH	We were talking about Benedict.
CLARISSA	He's treated us very badly.
GRACE	You admit that now. I knew he'd let us down.
RUTH	Grace, this has been very hard for Clarissa. She trusted Benedict.
GRACE	Didn't you learn when Jack left that you can't trust men. Even Stephanie knows that.
STEPHANIE	I trusted my granddad. He never lied to me.
RUTH	I trusted my George. We knew when we got married we'd always be together. Two is better than one he said.
CLARISSA	That's typical of you Grace, you don't trust anybody. Maybe it's time you did.
RUTH	We're all getting a bit overwrought.

	It's not our fault the shop is closing. And it's not Clarissa's fault that Benedict lied to her. We come here to help people not to be angry with each other.
GRACE	We come here because we need to. It's here we meet people and do things. And now it's going to end, because of Benedict the Bastard. I don't know what I'm going to do.
RUTH	I'm going to work at the food bank next week.
STEPHANIE	You'll see my mum there.
RUTH	Is she a volunteer?
STEPHANIE	No, it's where she gets our food.
CLARISSA	We'll miss you, Ruth.
RUTH	What are you going to do, Clarissa?
CLARISSA	I don't know, but I won't trust Benedict again.
GRACE	You never should have to begin with.
CLARISSA	He seemed so plausible, and the shop's been good for me.
STEPHANIE	Sounds like you're frightened.

CLARISSA	I just don't know what I'm going to do. I need this shop.
GRACE	You need the company.
CLARISSA	We can't just give up. I can't just sit at home all day and do nothing.
GRACE	At least your life's your own. I'm going to be stuck with Dennis and the bleeding telly.
STEPHANIE	What am I supposed to do, I'll get sent away.
CLARISSA	I'm sure they'll send you somewhere else, maybe Oxfam.
GRACE	You need a job, not this nonsense.
STEPHANIE	Nobody will give me a job.
GRACE	The bakery has a card in the window. They want a new assistant. You should go and see them.
STEPHANIE	They won't want me. I don't have any exams, I don't have any work clothes, I don't know about baking and selling things.
GRACE	Now it's you that sounds frightened.
STEPHANIE	I am frightened. I've never had a job.

GRACE	The hard thing about this is overcoming the fear. You don't need qualifications. What you do need is courage. Believe in yourself for once. What would your granddad say?
STEPHANIE	He'd tell me to go for it. But I haven't anything to wear.
CLARISSA	There's plenty of clothes here. You can help yourself to whatever you need.
RUTH	I'll help you choose some if you like.
GRACE	She doesn't want this rubbish. They all wear the same in the bakers. He'll give her a uniform.

Ruth exits to storeroom to collect the teapot.

STEPHANIE	What about the court? I'm supposed to be here.
CLARISSA	Don't worry about them; I'll sort it out.
GRACE	The baker is an old friend of mine. You go down there and tell him I sent you.
STEPHANIE	Okay, I'll go for it.

As she gets to the door she turns and Ruth re-enters the

shop with the teapot.

	Thank you.

Exit Stephanie.

CLARISSA	That was kind of you Grace. Do you think she'll get the job?
GRACE	Of course she will, she's a bright kid. She's just had a raw deal.
CLARISSA:	And you're off to the foodbank next week, Ruth.
RUTH	I start on Monday.
GRACE	You'll be able to tell them all about George.
RUTH	I don't know what you mean.
CLARISSA	Grace!
GRACE	Sorry Clarissa. You'll be great at the foodbank, Ruth.
RUTH	There's an induction for volunteers today. I'd like to go.
CLARISSA	Well off you go then.
RUTH	I'm taking the teapot with me. Goodbye then.

GRACE   'Bye

CLARISSA   Goodbye, Ruth, good luck.

Exit Ruth through shop door.

GRACE   Just you and me now. What are you going to do?

CLARISSA   I might go away for a bit. What about you?

GRACE   I've given years of my life to this shop, and it's all been for nothing. I don't know what I'm going to do now.

CLARISSA   I suppose you'll be looking after Dennis.

GRACE   I only ever came here to get away from him, but I've got no one else.

CLARISSA   You've got me, Grace.

GRACE   But you don't even like me.

CLARISSA   Of course I do. Look what you just did for young Stephanie. You've got a softer side that rarely comes out, but I can see it.

GRACE   I don't know what you're talking about.

CLARISSA	Yes you do. And there's others who need to see that side of you too.
GRACE	You're talking in riddles now. I don't know what you're on about.
CLARISSA	I'm talking about your son, his family, your grandchildren.
GRACE	That's cruel. You know I never see them.
CLARISSA	But you can now, I'll take you.
GRACE	What? To Australia?
CLARISSA	Yes, to Australia. I've travelled a lot. I know how all that works.
GRACE	But I can't do that. I've never been anywhere, I've never been on a plane, I've never even left this town.
CLARISSA	I'm sure you've got as much courage as Stephanie had when you persuaded her to go to the bakers. You do want to go and see him, don't you?
GRACE	Of course I do, but can we really do it?
CLARISSA	I don't see why not. We'll make it our project.

GRACE But what if he doesn't want to see me?

CLARISSA Does that matter, you'll see him.

A little silence

You know you have to do this.

GRACE Okay. What do we do now?

Clarissa bangs the till open and drops her keys inside and closes the till.

CLARISSA Now you lock up, with your keys.

Exit Grace and Clarissa through shop door.

Curtain

Performance

For information about performing rights and for performance scripts please contact Rik Lonsdale at rik.lonsdale@outlook.com

About the Playwrights

John Nash

As a young man John Nash published several short stories after winning a national competition for unpublished authors. Children and work intervened and he gave up his stories to write professional essays in trade journals. In recent years he has written a regular column in a local magazine making unlikely links between poetry and current events. He also admits to writing pantomimes for local consumption. Vintage is his first collaborative work of drama.
He lives in Dorset with his wife and an insensitive dog.

Rik Lonsdale

Rik Lonsdale's lifelong desire to write persisted through three previous careers and the raising of children. Eventually he was able to turn his energies to learning the art and craft of writing.
"Water and Blood", his first novel published in March 2023, was inspired by his concern for the future of civilisation and the human race.
"Morsels of Life", his first collection of short stories, shares his love of people, their humour, and humanity and was published in November 2023.
"Hotel", a novella, was published in July 2024 and explores the transactional nature of a relationship.
Rik lives in Dorset with his wife and an insensitive vegetable plot.
If you would like to know more about Rik and his writing journey you can find him at www.riklonsdale.com or on social media.

www.ingramcontent.com/pod-product-compliance
Lightning Source LLC
Chambersburg PA
CBHW060620080526
44585CB00013B/910